EARTH WOMAN

Tetyana Shvachuk

EARTH WOMAN

7 Levels To Awaken Your Beauty, Feminine Power, And Influence.

BALBOA.PRESS
A DIVISION OF HAY HOUSE

Balboa Press books may be ordered through booksellers or by contacting:

Balboa Press
A Division of Hay House
1663 Liberty Drive
Bloomington, IN 47403
www.balboapress.com
1 (877) 407-4847

Because of the dynamic nature of the Internet, any web addresses or links contained in this book may have changed since publication and may no longer be valid. The views expressed in this work are solely those of the author and do not necessarily reflect the views of the publisher, and the publisher hereby disclaims any responsibility for them.

The author of this book does not dispense medical advice or prescribe the use of any technique as a form of treatment for physical, emotional, or medical problems without the advice of a physician, either directly or indirectly. The intent of the author is only to offer information of a general nature to help you in your quest for emotional and spiritual well-being. In the event you use any of the information in this book for yourself, which is your constitutional right, the author and the publisher assume no responsibility for your actions.

Illustrations are done by Alexandra Tysozhna and cover photography by chillapalosh.com

Print information available on the last page.

ISBN: 978-1-9822-3672-4 (sc)
ISBN: 978-1-9822-3674-8 (hc)
ISBN: 978-1-9822-3673-1 (e)

Library of Congress Control Number: 2019916185

Balboa Press rev. date: 09/18/2020

"This book is dedicated to my parents Dr. Ivan & Raisa Shvachuk - who raised me to see beauty through my soul."

CONTENTS

INTRODUCTION

The ideas presented in this book started with my own challenges having been born a woman.

While I was learning about myself, I felt I didn't understand other women.

I wanted to know what made a woman beautiful. Were they the same things that made her happy too?

Our culture tells us to be one way, but what about what our soul tells us?

I didn't want to be a victim and blame men for everything gone wrong in my life. I didn't want to feel bitter and identify with women who wanted to be like the men they despised either.

I wanted to be free to define my own role as a woman, stripped of cultural pressures and prejudices.

The more I started to understand the topic of femininity, words and information started flowing through me.

I began to feel like I belonged. I was gaining confidence and felt secure from within. I didn't need material things to define me. I was powerful as a woman.

MY STORY

I was born in Ukraine, in the picturesque city of Ivano-Frankivsk. I had lots of friends and family surrounding me at all times. Life felt normal, until my family decided to move to the United States when I turned twelve.

We moved to live the American dream, although in the beginning it did not feel that way. Life was nothing like I dreamed of. Life was full of obstacles and hardships to overcome. There were many lessons to learn, and much to discover about my new culture.

After a while though, things improved, I found myself accepting my new life as an American teenager. I absorbed main-stream culture like a sponge. I wanted to fit in, but fitting in was never to be for me.

Like most American teenagers at the time, I preoccupied myself with the western approach to beauty, which meant obsessing about my weight, eating zero fat and using every beauty product out there. This approach only made me chubbier and more insecure. And needless to say, it made me unhappy.

I was picked on at school and would come home crying every day. My grades were top of the class, but my social life was close to zero. I still felt different and I was very sensitive.

At that point I turned inward and started to work on understanding why it was so hard for me to be friends with other girls. I also wanted to understand how beauty played into it all, as I was fascinated with anything associated with beauty.

That's why in college, I was so drawn to psychology, even though I was mostly taking pre-med classes like chemistry and biology. I became more and more fascinated with the mind and majored in psychology and biology.

After college, I started to spend more time in Ukraine. My new job as a journalist brought me back to my homeland. I liked being in Ukraine, because I was constantly inspired by the beauty around me.

The beautiful energy flowed from the women. They had this aura of radiance and confidence about them. It wasn't just outside beauty that was striking, it was something deeper. It was charisma and poise, and almost every woman seemed to possess it in her own unique way.

It made me wonder what was it that made every woman seem so beautiful in such a jaw-dropping way.

And whatever it was, I wanted to be the same. I wanted to know what made Ukrainian women so desirable and yet it all seemed so effortless.

I thought it must be genetics, but a closer look started to tell me something different. I zeroed in and realized that Ukrainian women practiced habits that made them beautiful.

Being away from this environment for many years, made it possible for me to see these patterns. I began to learn the art of beauty the Ukrainian way, digging into my own ancestral beauty secrets and traveling around Ukraine in a quest for knowledge.

As I was discovering how to understand beauty in a new way, I began to see results in myself. I was becoming more beautiful in every way. This made me think that, if I can do it, then these secret habits can be replicated by anyone who wishes to be beautiful.

But it did not end there. With beauty comes great power. And I am not talking about external beauty. It is the strength at the core of a woman that gives her the power beyond her imagination. I discovered this along the way - through old-world wisdom of generations before me.

It was the power of the Feminine Divine, the energy that started to flow through me as I learned to connect to my femininity. Through channeling and experience I learned the wisdom that helped me to live a life to its fullest potential. And that is what I will teach you in this book.

STRUCTURE OF THE BOOK

While writing this book, I felt compelled to use the chakra system as levels to interpret femininity and explain important concepts in an organized way.

By associating different parts of femininity with each chakra center/ level, I was able to create a system that you can easily remember and reference, as the concept of femininity cannot be easily explained in one sentence.

As you go through each level, you gain new skills and knowledge that will guide your journey to connect to your Feminine Divine. With every step, you get more in tune with your energy and what it means to be feminine.

The concept of chakras was born in India thousands of years ago. It is a way to describe the energetic body. The western world has been adopting the chakra system into its modern way of living for the past hundred years.

Carl Jung, a renowned psychologist who studied the chakra system and helped to weave its wisdom into western society, interpreted the meaning and created symbolism for each chakra that we now understand and use.

Abraham Maslow created his famous pyramid of hierarchy of needs, which in my opinion, closely resembles how the chakras are represented. The base of the pyramid identifies with our survival, the need for food and shelter. As you move up the pyramid, you become more self-actualized, meaning more connected to who you are and your Divine spirit.

The chakras work much the same. As we move up from the first chakra representing our basic needs and survival, we go up to higher chakras until we reach the connection with the source itself, where we find our soul's purpose.

HOW TO USE THIS BOOK

This is a channeled book, meaning it has been written as a download from my connection to the Feminine Divine Energy. Some things are repetitive by design, as one learns by repetition. Sometimes the subjects jump from one to another fairly fast. That is an inherent style of my channeled messaging.

This book is meant to be used as a reference throughout your life as issues arise. At any time you lose touch with who you are as a feminine being, you can open a chapter and bring yourself back.

Through the continuous practice of these principles, you will be able to heal your femininity blocks.

The exercises after each chapter will help you turn this inspired text into everyday practice. Each chapter helps to evolve different parts of your femininity, while each of those parts is interrelated with one another.

There is also a Feminine Energy Activation chart at the end of the book to help you look up the affirmations for each chapter in one place.

LEVEL 1

THE GATEWAY TO THE FEMININE DIVINE

Chakra: 1st, Root
Element: Earth
Color: Red

1ˢᵀ CHAKRA AFFIRMATIONS

"I am surrounded by women who love me and whom I honor."

"I am part of the natural world. It inspires and invigorates me."

"I connect to the Feminine Divine Energy by nurturing my body through food."

The first chakra, also known as the root chakra, is the foundation that supports our lives. It represents the roots we grow with our tribe. It is the nourishment we give to ourselves. It is also the first level to connect to your feminine power.

The energy of the first chakra represents our basic needs, our most primal necessities in order to survive. It is a place that makes us feel safe and secure. The place where we feel grounded and connected to the world around us, from which we grow our mental and emotional strength.

HISTORY OF THE FEMININE

In the feminine lies the beginning of creation. When we imagine the beauty that surrounds us, it is an expression of the feminine. We cannot live without it. Our world cannot run without constant creation of the feminine force.

Thousands of years ago, the feminine was worshiped and honored as sacred. Since then, it has been repressed, denigrated, and forbidden. It was made to be forgotten as a source of power for women, because of the fear that women would become too empowered and too hard to control.

3

Through repression, we forgot our true strength, but fortunately we kept a small thread weaving from generation to generation, protecting the connection to our Feminine Divine.

A flame within us that can never go out is getting reignited again. We are starting to wake up to that divine energy, reconnecting with its powerful alignment.

DEFINITION OF THE FEMININE

We live in a world that tells us to be a certain way despite it not serving us as women. We are constantly trying to break the glass ceiling, compete with men and other women and stay stuck in a vicious circle of disempowerment.

But we are waking up to our power now.

Over the recent years, more and more feminine movements have become prominent, but the society that we live in now is still struggling to keep up with our evolution as feminine beings.

The old narrative of feminism is to be like men, but the new narrative of feminism that is just beginning to spread its roots is to be a woman.

We need to fill the void in our hearts that left us deeply wounded from centuries of being oppressed, our powers taken away and our voices silenced.

So where do we start?

We can keep on trying to fight the system or we can build our own system that works for us: our own collective of the Feminine Divine that is more ready than ever before to be tapped into as the true power source of all that is.

The Feminine Divine is not all about being nice, weak or flowery. It is about compassion, self-love, nurturing, emotions, embracing highs and lows, self-acceptance, soft power, collaboration, intuition, gracefulness, and beauty.

Being a woman holds an incredible power and potential to change the world, shift our thinking from hate to love and to use our spiritual gifts to empower each other. That is the mission of a true Earth Woman, a warrior for love, beauty, harmony, and balance.

By tapping into the Feminine Divine Energy, a woman is 100 times stronger and more effective in everything that she does and everything that she is.

It is time for us to heal the world with femininity.

So what do I mean when I keep saying "Feminine Divine Energy?"

That is the space within ourselves that is filled with infinite beauty which feeds our feminine aura and brings all our talents and dreams to light. It whispers the right guidance for us to connect to our most beautiful self where we sparkle from the inside.

It is as if we are surrounded by pure bliss at all times, where nothing can distract us from our true and authentic self.

As a woman, this is our most powerful gift, and yet we often get confused and tap too much into the masculine energy.

Every woman has both masculine and feminine energies and I will cover this in more detail in the next chapter. Living in a male dominated society, it is very easy to be in masculine energies at all times, but this doesn't serve us well as women.

We are feminine beings and what we should know is that fully tapping into our feminine energies brings us closer to who we truly are and makes us feel empowered in the world we live in.

We live in a culture that tells us to be more masculine and aggressive. However, is that really necessary for our survival and growth? We are quite unhappy as women nowadays, and yet our standard of living is better than ever before.

It is not our socioeconomic status that brings us much pain and misery, but it is in fact our deep disconnect with our beautiful feminine energy.

We have forgotten how to be feminine. We have forgotten how to be what is most natural to us.

So how can we be truly happy and filled with love when we don't know how to find that within ourselves?

Femininity has gotten a bad rap over the years. It often represents an overly emotional unstable woman who cries all day. We think being feminine is weak and that no one will respect us.

Femininity is seen as an inconvenience, something to be ashamed of. We learn to be ashamed of our beautiful bodies, and our cyclical nature.

We pretend to be tough, when we should be sensitive. We try to hide our pain, bury it deep inside, so that we don't seem too emotional or unstable.

We are still focused on appeasing what is more comfortable for men, than doing what is truly good for us as women.

Men are not comfortable with tears, so we don't cry. Men do not understand monthly hormonal fluctuations, so we get labeled as crazy. Men get overwhelmed with our intellectual abilities, so we hide them.

We have learned to be dishonest about how we truly feel with men, because of the fear they might not understand our complexity.

This is a crisis of a global magnitude. We cannot keep existing in this way. We need solutions. We need change.

However, we cannot blame men for our problems as women. We LOVE men! We are allowing it to happen, because we are not in tune with who we are as powerful feminine beings.

So let us delve into what feminine power is really about. I have learned so much from Ukrainian women about what it really means to be feminine.

Just like French women know the secrets of great style and never getting fat while eating a diet full of butter, Ukrainian women are very connected to nature and strongly embody femininity. Having spent half of my life in Ukraine and the other half in the US, I have observed these women from a multi-dimensional lens and noticed that they have evolved with a better connection to the Feminine Divine. And that is what I am so excited to share with you in this book.

You see, Ukrainian women do not view femininity as a weakness like we do here in the US. Women in Ukraine are brought up knowing that being feminine is their most significant source of power and their birthright.

Of course, femininity and beauty have everything in common. The Earth in itself is a feminine being and thus creates the beauty that we can immensely admire and strive to realize.

Femininity is where your most beautiful self can come alive. It is the energy that nurtures a masterpiece that is you.

For example, we think of strength as a male trait, and thus define strength in a way that a man does. However, a woman has her own definition of strength and it is quite different from a man.

Strength defined in feminine terms is more beneficial for us to practice as women, because it is tailored for us, and not for men. What men perceive as weak, we hold as strength.

The Power of Emotion

Men are taught that controlling or repressing emotions is a sign of strength. This might work for men most of the time, because biologically men tend to have a lot of testosterone and very little estrogen. Testosterone is a hormone signifying male power, where strength becomes defined as high energy, non-emotional, and aggressive. Women are more estrogen dominant, which is a hormone responsible for our emotional and sensitive nature.

Now, if we as women take on the definition of a man's power, then we cut off our own supply of strength. Our own female tailored definition of strength somehow gets overlooked and underused. If we are trying to be tough and rough, like men, we become unhappy. Deep down we know it feels off, like something is not right with us. It just doesn't feel natural.

What does feel natural is our own definition of strength, and guess what? It is the complete opposite of male strength.

For women, showing emotion is showing incredible strength of character. Since we are estrogen-dominant, emotion is something that is essential to who we are. We thrive with emotion, where men can completely lose touch with themselves when they get too emotional.

A woman's strength is defined as an all encompassing emotional power house, but how we use this source of power is what makes us either strong or weak.

Because of our strong intuitive abilities, we have the potential to use emotion as a compass to navigate our lives. However, we have to gauge our emotions and recognize which ones are coming from the Feminine Divine and which ones are more male-oriented, such as jealousy (aggression) and toughness (not feeling).

Emotion is at the core of the very essence of being a woman and the most powerful source of true strength.

We must learn how to use our emotions to our advantage. For example, listening to that bad gut feeling when we first meet someone versus ignoring it and getting hurt later.

Or when we want to get our way in a relationship - instead of nagging and crying and playing the victim, we speak calmly and firmly yet be soft in our approach. Start with a compliment, because we are naturally wired to see the good aspects of people around us. We need to use our strength as women by tapping into our estrogen dominant nature.

Ukrainian women grow up learning the truth about femininity. They understand how much knowledge it holds. It is such a natural part of the culture.

The view of femininity in Ukraine is that of strength and courage. It means taking a leadership role in your life.

Being feminine means accepting yourself as a woman. It means taking responsibility for your own happiness and livelihood. It is loving who you are as an amazing and totally unique beauty.

SURVIVAL IN THE COLLECTIVE

We forgot a long time ago that a big part of being a happy woman is being part of a collective.

Where men get their power from the individualistic mentality, women get their strength from supporting and being supported by others. For example, when a man has a problem, he often wants to go to his "cave" and work it out alone. On the other hand, when a woman has a problem, she wants to talk it out with someone and express her emotions.

The idea of a complete and happy family of a couple with 2.5 kids is really just a mirage for the complex lives we live in.

Women need other women.

We have needs that extend beyond the family, sometimes we need understanding that no man can give us, but only other women can.

The times when femininity flourished, before Patriarchy dominated, women depended on a strong network of other women. They helped each other in every part of life, from child rearing to emotional support.

But today, we have forgotten about this structure. We think we can do it all, strictly relying on the concept of a "nuclear family" to fulfill all our needs.

And this is where the foundation cracks under the immense pressure of this isolationist mentality. We start to become unhappy, even though on the surface it would seem we have everything we need to be 'happy'.

Depression hits, relationships crumble, we lose control with our kids.

Nowadays more and more women are relying on antidepressants, yet the quality of our life is better than ever before. Antidepressants are just another bandaid over a bleeding wound. They only cover the symptoms, but do not address the root cause of the depression epidemic.

The truth is our lives are not working.

We are stuck in an old belief system that we only need one person, our husband, who is supposed to be everything to us. That one man is supposed to magically replace our mother, our sister, and our three best friends. That is a lot of pressure.

Then one day we wake up and we wonder why we are so unhappy. We are unhappy because we feel trapped in our unrealistic expectations about relationships, whether it is with our husband, kids, or a job... or all of them put together.

I am not saying, leave your family, and start a woman's camp. What I am saying is that it's time to change the structures that keep us from living the most fulfilling lives. And for that we need other women.

The problem is that living in a patriarchal society, we have learned to make women our enemies. And we will keep hating each other, because every potential woman to us is a threat, not a friend. Who wants to live in a world like that?

Together vs Against

The Patriarchy wants to keep us fighting against each other so we don't realize our power as women. It wants to keep us separated and silenced to diminish our value.

If we do not learn to love each other and be inspired by each other as women, we are going to keep living in a man's world, following men's orders.

How can we feel empowered if we disempower ourselves all day, everyday?

There is not a magic pill that suddenly gives us confidence that lasts. It takes deep work on ourselves and our attitude toward others.

When I am in Ukraine, I feel a sense of community among women. Women support and help each other to be better.

Women are nurturing, sensitive, and understanding by nature, yet we can be so vicious to each other. We can make nasty comments about other women, without even knowing them. Why are we so mean to each other?

It all stems from our own deep dissatisfaction within ourselves, our deep disconnect from the Feminine Divine.

We have not realized how magnificent and beautiful we all are.

We do not see the beauty of other women as part of our own beauty.

If we have the need to constantly deride one another, we do not understand that we belittle ourselves as a result.

By negatively reacting to another woman's success and beauty, we actually impair our own ability for the same.

Beauty will not grow from a place of fear and insecurity. That is not where femininity (beauty) thrives.

We must understand this concept. *By supporting other women, we are in fact nurturing ourselves.*

We are so focused on fighting inequality among men and women, that we have forgotten how much inequality we have within our own gender. It is something that only we, as women, are responsible for.

If we could, together, combine our strength that flows from our Feminine Divine Energy, we can heal the world from pain and violence, but instead we perpetuate and add to the problem.

When a woman taps into her Feminine Divine Energy, she has the power to create balance and harmony in her environment.

Imagine that a woman creates a community of women. She teaches them how to tap into their own Feminine Divine Energy. They then do the same and it spreads like wildfire: a creative force awakened from within.

Each woman helps another to thrive.

My story: Growing up, I felt shy and unable to express my emotions. I had childhood asthma, which made me extra sensitive and anxious about talking to others. It was a psychological side effect of sometimes not being able to breathe and being scared that it might happen when I get too emotional or hyperactive.

Because I wasn't able to express myself, it was hard for me to have girlfriends. Naturally girls bond by sharing secrets, feelings, and everything else that's going on in their lives, and I couldn't do that.

I wondered why I felt so easy around boys, where there was not much talking, but more climbing trees and planning out the next forbidden adventure. However, as I grew older my hormones kicked in and I had no choice but to embrace my emotional side.

It felt so uncomfortable at first. I felt like crying all the time. The world seemed like a traumatic place full of triggers that made me weep. My desire for having girlfriends also grew, as I opened up and released all the pent up emotions I was carrying.

The feminine side in me finally opened up and I felt home. It was like learning how to ride a bicycle. I experienced lots of falls, but the urge and freedom to ride was unstoppable.

GROUNDING FEMININITY IN NATURE

The depth of inspiration in feminine energy is infinite, as is our natural world. One way to develop our feminine side is to learn to connect to nature and its inherent femininity.

Let the beauty of flowers, the aroma of fresh air after the rain envelop you in a world of magic and serenity, so that you may find your own sacred space deep within.

Admiring nature in an intricate way allows you to become part of that beauty, to share that moment with admiration, and to awaken your beautiful spirit.

As the perfect representation of femininity, nature has the most soothing effect on us in the most alluring way.

Being one with nature and understanding the deeply profound effect it can have on your beauty is something Ukrainian women practice daily.

They like being outdoors in parks and forests, enjoying the fresh air and absorbing the wisdom of natural beauty around them.

Not only is this a spiritually meditative practice, but one that physically affects the way you look right away. The overabundance of oxygen that gets released from trees makes you look fresh and rejuvenated.

It is not hard to connect to nature, all we have to do is to surround ourselves with a green oasis and simply take part in nature's wonderland.

Observe the leaves whistling in the wind.

Take in the colors and natural fragrances abound.

Speak with the wildlife, the birds, the ants, the squirrels.

And when you take an active part in nature long enough, you get lost in the moment. A moment where you feel connected to everything that is in it.

This will accelerate your connection to Feminine Divine and grow your beauty.

This is what beauty is all about, because when we can take ourselves into nature, we develop an ability to take ourselves deep within in search of our own beauty.

When we are in awe of nature, we understand what beauty is about and the feelings it invokes within ourselves.

It brings our awareness of how beautiful we really are, that we are created in a perfect way and we should celebrate ourselves much like nature celebrates being alive.

The Earth has a profound effect on our stability. It is the floor beneath our feet, both literally and metaphorically speaking. It grounds us to feel secure and balanced.

When we connect to the Earth's energy, we feel more like our true selves. It is important to know that whenever we are at a loss and don't feel emotionally stable, we have the Earth's energy ready and available to heal and ground us.

In Ukraine, Earth has a very special meaning. It signifies the bounty of life. I've spent a lot of my childhood running around barefoot on the grass, but I had no idea how significant it was.

What I discovered later about walking barefoot was astounding. We are actually connecting to Earth's energy with the soles of our feet and it has a very healing impact on our bodies.

So now anytime I feel out of sorts, I walk barefoot on the grass, or on little rocks next to a river bank. It helps me connect to who I am and thus making me feel more beautiful.

Connecting to nature is a form of active meditation. It is a profound experience because it brings us closer to ourselves.

Whenever you feel fear and get stuck in a negative vibrational frequency, go out for a walk in the park, if the weather allows, do it barefoot. In very little time you will feel refreshed and rejuvenated. You will feel happier and more grounded, because nature has a way of cleansing your body, mind, and spirit.

Women in Ukraine truly understand that in order to be beautiful, we must allow the beauty from within to come out while filling ourselves up with the beauty of nature from the outside.

Our Feminine Divine Energy gets nourished by our connection to the outside world. When we seek to find beautiful surroundings and inspiring moments, we grow our beauty and feed our soul.

Our ability to fine tune ourselves to see beauty all around is what creates the beauty within.

Flower Power

What I love about Ukrainian culture is that women get flowers from men or other women as a celebration of their beauty. Women here in the US mostly get flowers when they are sick or dead, or when someone is apologizing. So flowers have a different meaning in these cultures.

I remember even when I was little, for my birthday party all the guests would bring me fresh flowers. The room was filled with flowers and it made me feel so beautiful and special. It made me so happy!

Women in Ukraine are used to getting flowers for all different occasions, and sometimes even when there isn't one. A flower is associated with a woman, her beauty and her divinity.

There are so many different flowers and they are all uniquely beautiful, like us women. It is such an inspiring association.

But in the US flowers are seen differently. Flowers do not have such a strong connection to the Feminine Divine. They are more like something to send as a thank you or as a sad reminder of one's bad times, but I do think that is also changing.

Flowers should be used for celebrating our femininity. Getting a beautiful bouquet of roses and tuning into their vibration of beauty will in fact make us more beautiful.

No one really enjoys flowers when they are dead. We want to appreciate them while we are alive.

In Ukraine women give flowers to other women. Who says we need to wait for men to get flowers? Why not inspire each other with beauty and our feminine desire to give?

My story: Whenever I want to feel more feminine, I go to a flower stand nearby and pick out what speaks to me at that particular moment. I bring flowers home and arrange them in a beautiful vase to admire for days.

This experience inspires me to feel more beautiful and reminds me that we are also like flowers, delicate and breathtaking. It also makes me think about how one must nurture oneself in order to blossom.

A flower craves sunshine and fresh water, much like we crave to be nourished by positive thoughts and meaningful emotional bonds.

In the spiritual world water represents emotion. It is what nurtures our roots and makes us grow and flower. Sunshine is warm, loving energy that heals and makes us whole.

Just like caring for a flower we must care for ourselves to make our true beauty come alive. We must admire ourselves in the mirror more often, whispering sweet words of love and affection.

All it takes is a beautiful word to brighten our day.

NOURISHING THE BODY

Part of nourishing ourselves is treating our bodies as a temple. A healthy spirit lives in a healthy body.

In order to connect to our Feminine Divine, we must learn to connect to our bodies. We must learn to really understand how our body works and what it needs in order to thrive. It takes the right mindset, proper nutrition, and being able to read our body's signals.

I have wonderful resources and articles that dive deep into this subject on my website earthwoman.me and social media, but for now let's go over some very important ideas.

It is a priority to have the right psychology about our body. If we are struggling with food addictions and imbalance, how can we focus on tapping into our true selves? How can we develop our true beauty, if we don't pay attention to our bodies first?

Our body is like a gateway to the world that surrounds us. The way we interact with the world is through our bodies. We use our senses to gain information that helps us to survive and thrive.

One of the most essential ways to connect to our femininity is through working on our bodies.

We want to create harmony and balance within, and that means treating our body with wisdom and respect.

This is where a holistic approach becomes integral to our wellbeing. Understanding the connection between mind, body, and spirit is what truly makes us feel whole and fulfilled.

In this chapter I discuss matters of the 1st chakra, our most basic needs as human beings.

Understanding our bodies and knowing what foods to eat in order to feel good, is our most basic need. There is so much information about this I can't wait to share, but is for a whole other book to come.

We often miss the signals our body is sending us, because we don't know how to listen.

To hear our body, we have to quiet all the noise around and turn up the volume on all the physical and emotional effects we feel at any given moment.

For example, your stomach is growling, because you skipped lunch. Instead of eating a proper meal, you get a coffee and keep going.

We often ignore our body, and override what it is trying to tell us, and then wonder why it doesn't function and look the way we want.

It is very important to find a different approach, where we take what our body is trying to tell us seriously. The more we listen, the more comfortable we feel in our bodies.

Part of listening to our body is also giving it proper nutrition. We must nourish our body with whole organic foods that are full of vitamins and minerals in order to thrive.

I can't stress this enough, knowing what to feed our bodies is vital.

It is vital on our journey to connect to our Feminine Divine Energy.

The main question to ask yourself every time you eat and drink is "Am I healing my body?" Or is what I am eating or drinking sabotaging my wellness?

When we take care of our basic needs from a place of nurturance and healing, we build a solid foundation on which we can build a beautiful life full of miracles and amazing possibilities.

LEVEL 1 ACTIVATION PRACTICE:

- CONNECT TO OTHER WOMEN (the COLLECTIVE)

  ☐ List 5 things you admire about another woman and reach out to her to tell her how you appreciate those qualities about her. It does not have to be all qualities at the same time.

  Name a woman _____

  1_____

  2_____

  3_____

  4_____

  5_____

  ☐ Ask a woman for help. Thank her sincerely without feeling an immediate need to return the favor.
  Name a woman _____

- BE IN NATURE

  ☐ Go out for a walk for 30 minutes without any technology and observe and interact with nature.
  Time scheduled to do it: _____

  ☐ Buy yourself a nice bouquet of flowers to celebrate the magnificent woman that is you.

- NOURISH THE BODY

  ☐ List five things that you can do to heal your body with food. Add them to your daily eating routine.

  1_____

  2_____

  3_____

  4_____

  5_____

  ☐ Start your meal with conscious gratitude for the food you are about to eat and think about how it will heal your body.

LEVEL 2

OUR TRUE SOURCE OF FEMININITY

Chakra: 2nd, Sacral
Element: Water
Color: Orange

2ND CHAKRA AFFIRMATIONS

"I honor the masculine and feminine energies within me."

"I love and respect men."

"I am a source of infinite beauty. It flows easily from me."

"I embrace my uniqueness, as it makes me beautiful."

"All I need is already within me."

The most powerful center for women is the place of the second chakra, or sacral chakra. It is the womb from which we create life. We give birth to our true identity here. It is the creative force that inspires everything in life, our vision of the world. This is the second level to activate your true power source, your Feminine Divine Energy.

By tapping into the energy of the second chakra, we build our relationships and our beliefs. We manifest our reality and acquire important lessons with and from others. We find the magic and beauty inside of us.

SPIRITUAL BEAUTY

Beauty is an energy flow, which has the power to be magnified by anyone who wishes to be enveloped in its magic.

If we can master the energy of beauty, we will always look and feel beautiful regardless of how much makeup we have on.

By learning how to tap into the infinite energy of beauty, not only will we evolve spiritually but our physical bodies will naturally change into a more pleasing form and appearance.

This is the most powerful way to achieve beauty.

Our true source of happiness is our ability to find our Spiritual Beauty.

When we allow ourselves to be filled up with all the ingredients of beauty, such as love, compassion, and confidence, we find the deep happiness that we longed for in our lives.

So what is Spiritual Beauty?

It is beauty that flows from the depths of our spirit where the very being of who we are resides in its most magnificent form.

When we find that magnificent self and learn how we can bring it into physical existence, this is when we are at our most beautiful.

We are conditioned to think that beauty has a certain set of standards - tall, blonde, skinny, but that is a truly narrow view of beauty.

Just like everywhere in the world, women in Ukraine come in different shapes and sizes, but what really makes them beautiful is their special feminine energy.

Why would we all be created so differently if God's view of beauty was just one perpetuating image? It just doesn't make sense.

Spiritual Beauty is not defined by the physical, it is the other way around. Who we are at the core of our being defines the beauty we possess.

By using this principle, we are in charge and it is up to us to discover the beautiful person we are already. *And the first step is to learn about ourselves as feminine sources of power.*

FEMININE VS MASCULINE ENERGY

The feminist movement in America and the rest of the world was a tremendous accomplishment for all women, but it is not over.

The way I see it is that the idea of feminism has to evolve into a new form that is tailored to women, not men.

Feminism brought about women who rejected their feminine nature in order to compete with men and be like men in order to be treated with equality.

How is this supposed to help us as women? We made the ultimate sacrifice of who we are as powerful beings and became more like men. No wonder it no longer works and we are still struggling for that 'equality.'

Today trying to be equal to a man is still playing by men's rules in a system created by men.

We are missing the point of feminism. Feminism should be about connecting to our Feminine Divine and not rejecting it.

The New Feminism manifests through femininity, not masculinity.

Our biggest source of power is in our feminine energy, the energy that has been stifled, abused, and hidden for too long.

The answer to our beauty lies in the feminine, because to be a beautiful woman we must be connected to our power source, the one and only Feminine Divine Energy.

We have been preoccupied for far too long with men telling us what is right for us and what we should look like. It is time to be who we truly are and shine our light brightly. Men will be the first to appreciate it, as men have been emasculated in the process of women taking on more masculine roles. Men too are suffering from this imbalance.

Diagram I: Masculine vs Feminine

Feminine Energy	Mascuine Energy
Compassion	Individualism
Self-love	Assertiveness
Nurturing	Being in control
Emotional depth	Go-Go-Go attitude
Collaboration	Aggression
Intuition	Power
Empathy	Decisiveness
Embracing highs and lows	Work till exhaustion
Self-acceptance	Taking action
Soft power	Ambition
Beauty	Independence
Gracefulness	Mono-tasking
Creativity	Competitive
Pleasure	
Letting go	
Multi-tasking	

We have been taught to take on male roles, yet we crave to be treated like women.

We need to tip the scales of dominant masculine energies that are not serving our needs and disempowering us as women.

Our world is in great distress from rampant wars to climate change. We are sinking as human beings and taking down our beautiful natural world with us.

We must realize that as women we have tremendous power to transform the world from calamity and destruction, and the only thing we have to do is to recognize how powerful we are as feminine beings.

We have forgotten ourselves as women because we so much wanted to be accepted by men.

We constantly give away our power by not being who we truly are, the creators of the life force.

Can we even comprehend the idea of how powerful we really are?

We hold amazing gifts as women, such as having great emotional depth and empathy, and yet we have been taught to reject these in order to succeed in a man's world.

We have been taught that we do not need much pregnancy leave when we give birth to a baby; we need to be ashamed of our periods; we need to have the same physical stamina as men. We need to have a career yet also create a family that our career path does not support. This contradicting world is happening because the rules were created by men for men. And as women we need to choose between evolving as an individual or having a family.

Why is it that we end up sacrificing so much to compete in a man's world?

Being a strong beautiful woman should not be about sacrifice, but about giving to the world the very things that make us special.

What our feminine energy holds are solutions to all our problems. It carries the blueprint to make our lives a true miracle.

Don't we think it is time to take our power back?

We have been through so much, and as a woman I can relate to being unhappy and feeling stuck, feeling like I have no control over my life.

There is another way of being, one that is living a life of purpose and true bliss.

And we can do that by learning how to connect to our Feminine Divine, our most significant source of power, all the time.

Think of this inner source, our Feminine Divine, as a constant energy supply that can feed all our needs and is always available.

We often rely on the outside for our source of energy in order to be happy and to feel beautiful. We depend on others for our own fulfillment. We feed our need for joy, beauty, power by seeking others' approval and attention.

I am not saying that we shouldn't build relationships with other people and connect with them, but most often we rely on others to give us our happiness. We may not do this intentionally, but as a cultural habit.

Consciously or not, we give our power away so that someone can decide for us when we should be happy and beautiful.

Instead, what we should do, is to learn to generate our own supply of happiness, joy, and beauty. This is the most important long-term way to create amazing beauty. It is like having our own well that is always there for our use.

My story: Spending my childhood in Ukraine, the roles for girls and boys were pretty classically defined back then. Girls played with dolls, while boys climbed trees and played sports.

I happened to have an older brother who had to take me everywhere with him (as per my mother's instructions to watch me), and so I learned to climb trees and do 'boys' stuff.

I still knew I was a girl though, and I liked that. It was like being part of a pack, but feeling special. All the things I couldn't do physically, like compete on their level of sports, didn't frustrate me, because it was strictly biological, and I understood that.

I didn't feel like I had to compete with them, I just really enjoyed their attention. I knew I was different, but not in a bad way. It was just part of nature. I didn't hate them for being boys or being stronger than me.

In Ukrainian culture, boys embraced being boys and girls embraced being girls. There were differences, but not everywhere, for example at school I was never treated any differently. I was just a student like any boy or girl and my merits solely depended on myself as an individual.

What I learned from my childhood was that boys are different and it's normal. I didn't need to prove that I was the same, I knew that I had my own strengths and uniqueness to take pride in.

THE INSIDE-OUT EFFECT

So how do we do it? First, we have to change our thinking. We are used to seeing the world from the "Outside-In" but, to find our Feminine Divine Energy, we must look within. Let me explain how.

True beauty has a different rhythm, and requires a different kind of mindset. If we want to help create new beauty within us, we must first grasp the idea of the *"Inside-Out Effect."*

This is the method that Ukrainian women use to create their beauty. They know that strengthening inner beauty is the most effective way to generate charisma, allure, and also physical beauty that lasts.

As we mentioned earlier, we are conditioned to think about beauty flowing from how the outside sees us - the *"Outside-In Effect."*

However, this only works short term and we become hooked on finding new ways to feel more secure, happy, and beautiful. Instead of feeling whole, we soon feel empty. As a result we try to get more things, focusing on a quick fix that leaves a deeper void from within.

We are not connected to our center. It doesn't matter how much 'stuff' we get, we develop feelings of not being enough, depression, and low self-esteem. This takes us even further away from being happily fulfilled and in touch with our soul's truest desires. We start to feel broken and depleted.

What our soul craves is not connected to our mind. Our minds tell us one thing, but our soul is never satisfied and we feel stuck.

We have been programmed to think this way, to consume for fleeting pleasure. Imagine if your soul was satisfied deep within. How many things would you actually need?

When we focus too much on the outside, we run away from ourselves. Don't get me wrong, I love buying beautiful dresses and makeup, but it is not what fulfills me and I am conscious of it, even when I wasn't before.

Now I buy one dress instead of twenty to inspire me, but not to make me happy. I am happy whether I have the dress or not, it does not define me. What defines me is what I nourish from the inside.

True beauty gets created from the inside and flows to the outside. *This means that beauty moves from inside out and that is the only sustainable way of feeling happy and beautiful.*

Diagram II: The "Inside-Out Effect" vs. "Outside-In Effect"

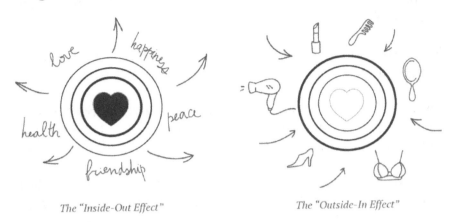

The "Inside-Out Effect" *The "Outside-In Effect"*

This is a very important concept to grasp for evolving Spiritual Beauty.

We cannot be complete without this part of beauty, no matter how physically attractive we are. Physical beauty is meaningless when we are not aware of our full spiritual potential. It becomes almost like a curse.

We all know women who seem to have the perfect body, face, looks, but are still unhappy or downright miserable. We think that if only we looked like her, we would be happy, but there are plenty of people who are unhappy and they seem to have it all.

For us to be happy, we need to realize that we have everything we need - and it's on the inside. And that is a habit that we are not used to cultivating. We have become so good at serving others, that we focus on everyone else but ourselves.

But we already have what we are looking for. All we need to do is to know how to unlock that wisdom. And I will show you exactly how to do it.

Unique Beauty

To connect to our Feminine Divine Energy, we must recognize that we have this special and unique beauty deep within that is waiting to be discovered.

What we hold, no one else has, and that is what makes us special.

Learning to appreciate our unique qualities and sharing them with the world can truly make us the most beautiful.

Life would be so boring if we were all the same, so why wish to be like someone else when we possess such an amazing beauty of our own?

My story: When I moved to the United States, I was teased a lot for being different. I felt insecure about everything, how I looked, spoke, acted. I valued myself based on the outside, I let my peers define me.

Later as a young adult, I tried to fill a void with material things and used shopping to soothe my deep dissatisfaction in life. It only made me more insecure.

I knew I had to find a better way. I could no longer pretend to be happy, I wanted to feel true bliss.

I could no longer participate in a culture of women hating other women. I wanted so much to live in a world where women inspired other women and helped each other find the strength to pursue their life's mission.

And most importantly, I wanted to feel whole, without the need to constantly prove to others that I was enough. I just wanted to be me, and that was all I needed to be happy.

Hence, this book was born from my own journey of learning how to connect to the Feminine Divine, and the many struggles and triumphs along the way.

Each woman holds the choice to either connect to her Feminine Divine that will empower her, or to keep being stuck in a cycle of an insecurity-driven life.

LEVEL 2 ACTIVATION PRACTICE:

- CULTIVATE FEMININE ENERGIES

  ❏ From the "Diagram I: Feminine vs. Masculine Energy" earlier in this chapter, identify the feminine and masculine qualities you have. In the first column, write the ones you want to keep and work on. In the second column, list the ones you want to let go of.

Qualities I want to work on	Qualities I want to let go of
_____	_____
_____	_____
_____	_____
_____	_____
_____	_____

❏ In order to strengthen your understanding of Feminine and Masculine energies, please put a checkmark in the appropriate column for each action.

Activity	Masculine energy (M)	Feminine energy (F)
1. Pushing yourself very hard		
2. Taking a luscious bath		
3. Getting a facial		
4. Making or keeping appointments you don't want		
5. Driving fast in a convertible		
6. Always deciding what you want and sticking to it no matter what		
7. Comforting friend's emotional pain		
8. Being right and defending your opinion just for the point of winning		
9. Forced self-care because it's on your to do list		
10.Looking at yourself in the mirror and lovingly listing your beautiful features		
11. Doing something for your own pleasure		
12. Trying not to cry, even if you feel like it		

Correct answers: 1M, 2F, 3F, 4M, 5M, 6M, 7F, 8M, 9M, 10F, 11F, 12M

- FOCUS ON UNIQUENESS AND SPIRITUAL BEAUTY ("INSIDE-OUT EFFECT")

  ❏ List 5 things that you do that make you happy inside and that inspire you. Schedule 30min-1h intervals for them in your calendar in the upcoming weeks.

    1_____

    2_____

    3_____

    4_____

    5_____

  ❏ List 10 things that you like about yourself or that you do well that make you unique. Every time you don't feel beautiful or you want to criticize yourself, read the list.

    1_____

    2_____

    3_____

    4_____

    5_____

    6_____

    7_____

    8_____

    9_____

    10_____

LEVEL 3

BUILDING BEAUTY THAT LASTS

Chakra: 3rd, Solar Plexus
Element: Fire
Color: Yellow

3ᴿᴰ CHAKRA AFFIRMATIONS

"I feel good therefore I am beautiful."

"I empower myself by living from a place of kindness and treating others the same."

"I find better ways to deal with life upsets."

The third chakra, or solar plexus chakra, represents honoring ourselves. It is how we understand our real power, and how we gain confidence. From this place we learn how to treat ourselves and how to be treated by others. On this third level we can build beauty that lasts.

Our self-esteem is built here by learning to understand our value. The truth of who we are, how we deal with the outside world, and our will-power all come from this energy center.

"FEELING", NOT "LOOKING"

The biggest misconception about beauty is that it is 100% genetics. It is still a common belief today. But I've spent years working on a different theory.

Growing up in Ukraine, there wasn't a big beauty industry. It was not a capitalist society - it was a communist one. Everyone had the same things and had to make do with what they had.

People drove the same cars and bought the same furniture and clothes, if these items were in stock, that is. Most of the time we had to wait for months to get a TV or a fridge. I am not speaking of some super distant past...these were the 80's.

The reality was that people had money, but there was nothing to buy. Ukraine was closed off from the world of international goods and information.

Does that mean beauty did not exist in Ukraine? It had considerably much less of the western type of beauty experience of creams, magazines, and a plethora of fashion.

No, quite the contrary...beauty flourished in Ukraine, all without lotions and potions. Ukraine had a culture of beauty, but not in a beauty magazine kind of way.

The beauty that I was surrounded with came from the inside. It was the kind of beauty that flowed like an energy force and permeated everything around with its feminine allure. The products, the lipstick, the fashion...it all came as an afterthought.

The main beauty, as I came to realize, is one of infinite capacity and comes from the spirit.

Women in Ukraine embody Spiritual Beauty, and it makes them very beautiful in a physical way.

If you had to live in a world where everyone had access only to the same things, how would you individuate yourself?

This is what Ukrainian women learned to master: how to stand out in a world whose sole purpose was to erase their identity.

It is easy to pick out an outfit and put on some makeup and feel like a whole new person, but that is only tapping into 20% of your beauty.

There is an incredibly rich world deep within us that we do not even realize exists.

More often than not, we are conditioned to believe in beauty through a cultural lens. Our perception of beauty is based on the ideas that others infuse into our being since our first spoken word.

For example, when a baby girl is born, everyone adores her and describes her in terms that relate to female beauty. Cute, princess, beautiful are attributes often used to impart the importance of physical beauty early on. So, in a way, beauty is not so much genetics as it is a cultural norm.

What is considered physically beautiful differs across the globe, but we can all agree that there is an underlying idea of beauty that transcends through time and space.

And what if I told you that you can tap into that beauty? The beauty that can make you beautiful on a universal level, not just a cultural one.

Anywhere you go, you would be considered beautiful, if only you knew one simple truth about beauty.

Beauty starts with how we feel, not how we look.

Our guide to understanding beauty starts with developing a barometer of how it makes us feel.

When beauty creates a sense of inspiration, hope, and motivation, we are on the right path.

However, if it makes us feel like we are not enough, then it will only deepen our dissatisfaction and hinder the real beauty that we hold deep within.

Fashion magazines are a great example of this.

If we open Allure magazine, we see lots of models with pretty clothes and makeup, and it can leave us very self-conscious.

If we view the magazine from a place of low self-esteem, it will only magnify our unworthiness, because all we're doing is comparing ourselves to a pretty picture.

Our minds are not focusing on the real truth, that it's just an image that was created in a laboratory of stylists, makeup artists, retouchers, and editors.

We are not taking the image for what it is, a piece of creative work; we are projecting our own insecurities onto it.

Our reaction to any kind of media, whether it be a novel, a magazine, an artwork, a movie, or social media, is only a reflection of our inner world.

By not accepting responsibility for our own happiness, we give our power away to someone or something else.

What if our feelings inside were that of confidence and love?

How differently would we view a glossy page of bright colors and the latest trends? We would be delighted to immerse our senses in a pretty picture, because the image would inspire our confidence and make our creative juices flow.

Beauty & Habits

Beauty reflects the state of our inner being.

If we consciously work on our inner state, if we choose to feel confident and inspired by beauty, no matter what we see, it will be a source of inspiration.

The art of beauty is just as complex as a science. It is too simple to say that some people are born beautiful and others are not.

What I have discovered in my own life goes against the mainstream idea of beauty. In fact, we are all born with a gift of beauty and we hold the power to make it come alive.

We can capture and evolve beauty, much like learning a new language, because each and every one of us is born with beauty we can create and bring out.

Through developing new habits, thought patterns, and connecting to our beautiful spirit, we release insecurities, unworthiness, and a lack of self-esteem. We will practice these principles in the next chapters.

We need to cultivate a sense of love for ourselves that will not only transform us on a deep spiritual level, but also a physical one.

Beauty is a set of habits - both physical and mental.

We might not be thinking of beauty as a set of habits, but if we consider, for example, brushing our teeth, that's a habit that helps our physical beauty.

There are two types of habits, the ones that take away our beauty and the ones that add to our beauty.

Throughout this book we are learning to identify and develop habits that dramatically add to our beauty, thus increasing our femininity.

CONFIDENCE STARTS WITH KINDNESS

We must nourish our emotional wellbeing by doing more of what we love and doing less of what we don't. When we redirect the focus from the outside noise inwards and listen in to our heart's desires, we create happiness from within.

Another way to tap into our Feminine Divine Energy is by monitoring how we engage with the outside world. How do we treat others? Do we feel negative about things or take on other people's negativity easily?

We are constantly affected by other people's energy, and much of the time this energy is negative. How you respond to that directly affects the flow of your beauty.

When we feel negative, we tend to be unkind and not understanding of others and ourselves. We can be judgmental and unforgiving, and when we are in that state, we block ourselves from our own beauty potential and feminine energy.

No matter how beautiful a woman may look on the outside, if she does not have kindness and love in her heart, she will not transcend her beauty to another level.

She will not be able to affect others in a profound way. She will not attract her desired mate.

When we treat others like the beautiful beings they are, we connect to our true energy deep within. At the same time, if we choose to connect to the negative parts of others, that is the energy we amplify within ourselves.

I observed that women in Ukraine are brought up to be kind and nurturing. They are understanding and compassionate towards others, which in return feeds their feminine energy and makes them more beautiful.

This is a revolutionary concept: Confidence for women starts with KINDNESS.

My story: Because I was a very sensitive person and an empath since birth, I had a hard time shielding myself from the negative emotions of other people. I would feel heavy energy after being around an angry or sad person.

At the time I was not aware that these were not my energies, but I knew that something was off, because naturally I have always had a very light and positive disposition.

So the way I learned to keep my positive energy constant was by being aware of how I felt at any moment and remaining present with myself even when there was a lot of negativity around me. When I became aware of this pattern, it became much easier to stay confident and secure.

When I was able to stay in my energies, I was able to transform other people's negativity by showing empathy and compassion. This made me confident and wanting to continue being kind even in the most unwelcome circumstances.

There is a greater purpose to being a caring human being. It is not just because it is the right thing to do, but it is the very thing that makes us beautiful.

If we truly want to be beautiful, we must practice kindness and love towards one another, because in order to grow we must give. That is the nature of our universe. By giving of our true selves we also receive love and nourishment back.

We are in charge of our beauty flow.

Women in Ukraine are also very giving in nature. They take care of everyone lovingly. They don't think that giving takes away something from them. They have this sense of honor to nurture others, because they recognize it as a gift they are born with.

We as women have the gift of Divine Feminine Energy. In order to tap into it, we must share it.

Think of this as a well beneath your house. When you use your well, the water flows. When you stop pumping the well, it will dry out. If you use too much water from the well in a short period of time, it will also dry out.

We must monitor the well for a constant flow, like our powerful divine energy.

Do What You Are Good At

The way to keep our feminine flow constant is by being confident about how we feel and what we do.

Confidence creates magnetism and allure. It is such an important aspect of beauty.

Most of us grow up without learning to be confident, and are more adept at being self-conscious. And it is not surprising, because we live in a Photoshop perfectionist culture.

How can we be confident if we don't fit into one universal standard of beauty?

How do we feel beautiful, when our beauty is different from what is considered beautiful by the media?

The answer is, we look inside ourselves and set up our own standards of beauty!

Nothing will make us more confident than when we own our beauty through and through. When we are in total control of our well-being and how we want to see ourselves.

Being confident is believing that what we have is of high value.

I learned many of these confidence secrets from Ukrainian women. The way they carry themselves is inspiring.

Ukrainian women are so feminine that it makes them strong and creates the ultimate confidence. This confidence is built around being proud of how they look, feel, and what they have accomplished.

We all have something that we are really good at, and that gives us confidence, because it feels natural and effortless.

That is the secret for creating confidence: Doing what you're good at.

Comfort Is The Compass

When we feel natural and comfortable in our own skin, confidence becomes a by-product.

If we want to be confident, we have to be aware of how comfortable we are.

The way to become confident is to be aware of how comfortable we feel and follow that good feeling.

It is a muscle you can stretch through practice. Ukrainian women practice being confident by simply being open to learning things they do not yet know, without overthinking how they appear as they learn.

Confidence comes with practice and patience, but the process is helped by imitating body language and behaviors that are associated with it.

For example, if you slouch and walk looking down, you will naturally create a state of uncertainty in your body. However, if you have your head up high and back straight, your body language displays boldness and power.

Being aware of your own body and adjusting it to a confident manner is a simple way of getting an instant boost of confidence.

Imitation As Betterment

At times when we lack confidence, being around a very confident woman can make us feel insecure, to a point that we feel threatened by it.

We need to let go of our fears, and admire the confidence of someone else. That way we will naturally pick up their confidence and become more secure ourselves.

Human beings are amazing at imitating other human beings. We are wired that way.

Surround yourself with what you admire and whom you want to be like, because in the long term you will end up being just like them.

Our natural reaction is to feel safe and secure, so we might choose to hang out with people who make us feel that way. However, if we want to improve and grow our beauty, we need to get out of our comfort zone, and that means hanging out with someone better than us.

That means making friends with people we are envious of, but secretly admire.

Do not be afraid to sometimes feel inadequate around those who are prettier, smarter or more successful than you. The more you hang out with them, the more their talents and confidence will rub off on you.

Ukrainian women are open and very happy to have friends who are more beautiful than they are. *The more they compliment and admire them, the more secrets they can learn for themselves.*

So why waste your energy on being jealous? It is not going to get you anywhere. Your mission should be "How do I improve?"

We need to bring the focus back to ourselves and ask what emotions will serve us best in any given situation. Let's not be so reactive to our insecure feelings.

This all goes back to being aware of ourselves, our bodies and our fears. Because once we are aware, we can use that information to our advantage by quickly adjusting to a better state.

Stay With The Logic

Confidence is also about paying attention to ourselves. We feel confident when we get a compliment, so why not give that compliment to ourselves when we most need it?

Have you ever noticed how sometimes you look in the mirror and see yourself as this beauty and the next day you look at yourself again and see something totally different? The perfect example would be saying, "I look good today," and the next day you're saying, "I look fat today."

If we really think about these two statements, physically there is no way that you can be great one day and suddenly feel like you have gained 20lbs the next day. It is just a perception of our minds that creates this disassociation, because physically we cannot change so quickly.

The good thing is that we can fix our minds to work in our favor and not against us. This can happen with an instant change of thought.

By catching our automatic mind habits that tell us one thing today and another tomorrow, we can become aware and rewire ourselves to think logically. If we felt beautiful yesterday, then it must be true today we are still beautiful.

Beauty cannot fade where it is appreciated and nurtured with kindness, but it will wither quickly where there is hate and constant criticism.

To build consistent confidence, we must control our minds from reaching such illogical conclusions about ourselves. In this way, we will create more beauty and fulfillment in our lives.

Learning to master our minds is vital in order to feel confident and happy, and I will explain this in more detail later on.

When we master this control and exercise it constantly, we open a dialogue that is kind and loving to ourselves.

STRESS AND BEAUTY

We stop the flow of beauty when we let life's stressors get to us.

Imagine your significant relationship has become too much to bear. You start to get depressed, because you don't feel like you can find a way to fix that relationship. Your life loses its luster, and you cannot find a way out. You fall deeper into depression.

When we feel helpless, we tend to get down and blame ourselves, which only creates a vicious cycle of self-hatred. We don't ask for help when we really need it. We think we can handle it, but sometimes we just cannot. Life becomes too much and we forget the joy that it should bring us.

We shut down, we hide away, we try to become invisible.

We all know how stressful life can be. If we let the stress take charge in our lives, it becomes a habit that is hard to get rid of. Our bodies start to get used to all that adrenaline rush, we start to crave it unintentionally.

Stress is an addiction. It is a way of being in your head all the time, playing the same stories over and over. It is like a trance that keeps you stuck in a negative pattern of thinking, creating a state of unawareness.

When we are unaware, we simply cannot get in touch with our beautiful selves, and we don't see the beauty around us.

When we are too stressed and rushed, we don't notice who we truly are. We forget to connect to our Feminine Divine Energy. We become robots programmed to go through life without experiencing the purpose of what we came here to do. We get so lost in the noise of our minds that we don't hear our incredibly beautiful souls.

When we let stress run our lives, we lose the beauty of any given moment.

Our focus is no longer on enjoying our lives, but it is on trying to control what we cannot.

However, we don't have to fall into these negative patterns that society throws at us, we can choose another way.

There is a way to deal with stressful situations without getting sucked into the negativity and energy draining drama.

Imagine not being affected by the chaos around you. Imagine feeling peaceful and content even when everyone else is not.

When you are centered around your core being, you can reject the conventional way of dealing with stress such as worry, panic, exhaustion or fear, and create a different habit instead.

We need to get into a habit of getting in touch with our greater purpose in life.

We should not waste our energy on daily stressors that inevitably take the attention away from honoring who we are.

We are often quickly reactive to what happens to us. We get angry at people when we shouldn't, we project the worst, we envision bad outcomes.

Instead, we need to step back and ask the question, "Is reacting this way going to help me get to where I want to be?"

"If I get angry or depressed, am I going to build what it takes to be beautiful and happy?" The answer is no, that road is not going to lead you where you truly want to go.

Yet so many times we unconsciously choose to react to situations in such a way that keeps us locked into a negative pattern.

For example, when we watch the news, which is almost always negative, we soak up all that bad energy that makes us angry and upset, even when everything is fine in our lives.

I am not saying that we should stop expressing our emotions. Instead, we must develop a radar to tell us which emotions do not serve our greater good.

If we keep absorbing life's stressors that are not our own, we can burn out in no time and have no positive energy left to make our life a beautiful one.

Thus, how we deal with stress on a daily basis determines whether we can open up our beauty from within. If we are preoccupied with being stressed, we are not in control of our mind, which may lead us to create unhealthy patterns of behavior.

LEVEL 3 ACTIVATION PRACTICE:

- CREATE BEAUTY BY FEELING IT

  ☐ Whenever you don't feel beautiful, remember that beauty is a feeling. You can change that feeling in a matter of a few seconds by focusing on what makes you feel good. And once you feel good, you will feel beautiful.

  Write 5 thoughts that make you feel beautiful:

  1_____

  2_____

  3_____

  4_____

  5_____

❒ As I mentioned, there are habits that "add to beauty" and there are habits that "take away from beauty." To practice this principle, please check in which category these habits belong:

Habits	Adding to beauty (A)	Taking away beauty (T)
1. Walking in nature		
2. Looking in the mirror and seeing only flaws		
3. Responding negatively to a compliment someone gave you		
4. Being happy for a friend because she got her dream job		
5. Only accepting parts of yourself that you like		
6. Caring for everyone you love, but forgetting about yourself		
7. Saying yes to commitments when you want to say no		
8. Taking the time to plan your meals in advance		
9. Finding a hobby that nurtures your soul		

Correct answers: 1A, 2T, 3T, 4A, 5T, 6T, 7T, 8A, 9A

- BUILD CONFIDENCE WITH KINDNESS

  ❑ Next time you are intimidated by someone at a mixer or social gathering, be open to getting to know them, smile and be warm. List three nice things you can say to a person you feel intimidated by. When you change your focus from yourself and your own insecurities, you distract yourself and flow into a more positive state.

  1_____

  2_____

  3_____

- CATCH YOUR STRESS PATTERNS

  ❑ When you notice an automated reaction to an outside trigger that makes you feel angry or upset, bring awareness back to yourself and ask: "How do I feel right now?" And what is it within me (old traumas, hurts, wrong-doings) that is making me react that way?

  Write a few examples of what comes to mind. Awareness is key.

Trigger	Reaction	Possible Reason
Ex: Husband saying "Can't you just..."	Anger & frustration	Feeling inadequate or not enough in childhood
_____	_____	_____
_____	_____	_____
_____	_____	_____
_____	_____	_____
_____	_____	_____

❒ List five ways you can be proactive and not reactive. For example, express calmly your intent in a positive way. Give the other person the benefit of the doubt that it might have been a miscommunication.

Stressors　　　　　　　　**Proactive Reaction**

_____　　_____

_____　　_____

_____　　_____

_____　　_____

_____　　_____

LEVEL 4

FEMININITY LIVES IN THE HEART

Chakra: 4th, Heart
Element: Air
Color: Green

4ᵀᴴ CHAKRA AFFIRMATIONS

> "I go through life from a place of love."
>
> "I love and accept myself exactly as I am."
>
> "When I do _____ (fill in the blank), I feel
> happy and I also choose to feel it now."
>
> "My own needs matter. I choose to do what makes me feel good."

The most powerful of emotions, love, rules the fourth chakra, which is also known as the heart chakra. In this fourth level we tap into our emotional selves, find balance from within, and discover how to live from a place of love.

It teaches us about the power of our emotions and how to use them to gain strength. It is a place of developing compassion and forgiveness, while learning to let go of negativity and fear.

Our heart is the gatekeeper to our soul and our amazing potential. It is an honorable place, full of integrity. It leads us to make choices that are in our highest good and that do not hurt others. It is a place of abundance and divine love.

When we let our minds run the show, our ego gets in the way, so it is hard to make the right decision. Yet when we lead from our heart, we always know what to do.

The more we are connected to our hearts, the stronger our intuitive guidance becomes.

For example, let's say we have an important decision to make like breaking up with a person who is not right for us. When we use our minds, we think about what everyone else is going to say or how that person might react. Our mind starts buzzing with "what if's" and we struggle, delay, and are afraid to make a decision.

When we look at the same situation using our heart, all the ego-driven chatter falls away, and our choice becomes about our true desire. We need to learn to open our hearts to our true potential and lead with our highest integrity.

When we lead from our heart - the place of deep connection to who we are - our physical and spiritual beauty shines through much stronger. When we stay in our head, our beauty gets limited in its expression.

BEAUTY LIVES IN THE POSITIVE

Spiritual Beauty involves learning how to love ourselves unconditionally, something we usually do not know how to do.

How much time do we spend in a day telling ourselves positive, loving thoughts? And how much are our thoughts self-hating or negative?

We are so used to putting ourselves down, that we don't even notice it anymore.

The only way to true beauty is through loving ourselves first. This means loving our unique spirit and what it came here to share with the rest of the world.

When we learn to accept ourselves unconditionally, we get to a place that is whole and free.

We release worry, fear, and caring too much about what people think of us. We know how beautiful we really are and how much love we have to give.

We know we have an unlimited potential that we can share with others.

By replacing negativity with positivity and connecting to the Feminine Divine, suddenly our life transforms to that of beauty.

It's easier to see your own beauty when you view things from a positive place. Beauty vibrates on a high frequency, so by staying positive we can tune in and connect to it.

Yet we have been conditioned to think otherwise. We have been made to think insecure thoughts about ourselves, our bodies, our beauty. We've been made to feel we are not enough, that we need to look like someone else to be perfect.

We are used to tuning into lower vibrations of lack when we think about beauty, but we will not find beauty there.

Beauty does not exist on the same frequency as anger, hate, and fear.

So how can we be beautiful, if we are entrapped in a negative mindset? We simply cannot.

FINDING YOUR EMOTIONAL WELLBEING

We have been taught to think of our emotional capabilities as women as a weakness. *But in fact, if we understand and evolve our emotional depth, we will find that it is one of the strongest and most powerful aspects we hold as women.*

We live in a busy and distracting world. Our senses are bombarded with products, experiences, and a lot of information. We get so distracted with the things outside of us, that we forget to check on our own emotional wellness.

And what do we mean by emotional wellness?

It is our internal compass for gauging the external world. It can be either love or fear-based.

What we must do is to consciously readjust our energies from fear, anger, and depression, to that of love and acceptance.

The more we are able to take hold of our emotions and transmute them into love, the more we feel in control without the need for toxic substances and other negative behavior patterns.

Acceptance

The way to change our emotions starts with practicing kindness towards ourselves and others.

This means accepting ourselves for everything that we like and everything we don't like.

Welcoming all the parts of our persona leads us to a stronger connection with the Feminine Divine Energy.

There are things that we dislike about ourselves and most of the time we focus on them hoping that they will disappear. However, what we focus on grows.

The best thing to do is to accept all of you, no matter how you feel about it.

It is very liberating to be at peace with the good and the bad. As soon as we do that, the parts that we hate about ourselves become easier to bear, until they are transformed completely.

When we know ourselves to be perfect in the present moment, that we are not broken, and don't need to be fixed, something amazing happens. We become our true selves.

This is why it is so important to accept ourselves for who we are. We need to learn to enjoy ourselves now, not when we get that amazing body, or a hot new boyfriend.

How often do we put off being happy as women? We think that "When I get to look like the girl on a magazine cover, then I will be happy."

The truth is, we won't be happy in the future, if we are not happy right now.

Instead of deriding our bodies and being hard on ourselves, we must stop and notice everything that is **right** with us. This is what I mean by being positive. It is the way to build a better relationship with the most important person, that is You.

Putting Yourself First

Accepting yourself also means that you put your basic needs first. We have been conditioned to believe that thinking about ourselves first is selfish, but how can we take care of anyone else if we don't take care of ourselves?

What kind of example are we setting for our kids, our family, our friends, when we put our basic needs last? We become used and underappreciated, because that is how we treat ourselves to begin with.

We tend to think that our basic needs as women are similar to those of men. However, our needs are not the same, they are quite opposite.

Women, as opposed to men, function from a much more emotional place. Our way of decompressing is to talk to a girlfriend over some nice tea and cake. We find solace in an emotional release, where men do the opposite. They need to decompress by detaching and not focusing on their emotions, such as by watching a football game.

It is very important to understand these differences and what works for us in order to replenish and renew our emotional wellbeing.

We have all seen a woman who has not been taking care of her emotional self. It may have been you at times. When she doesn't take the time to release and renew, she has a hard time managing her emotions and can become harsh, abrasive or extremely sensitive.

Our emotional balance goes haywire when we do not give to ourselves in a nurturing and kind way. We can run ourselves into the ground doing favors and laboring for our family or at work. We expect that their appreciation will be a way to replenish our energy supply and emotional wellbeing, but this doesn't work. We try to fill ourselves up from the outside, expecting others to know what we need.

This kind of cycle continues until we are left burned out and unhappy, because we are too busy focusing on the needs of others before our own.

We are left angry and resentful at the people whom we feel we serve.

This pattern shuts off the love that we are able to feel and give to others, and thus creates the perfect atmosphere for negativity to thrive.

However, life does not have to be this way if we learn to truly love ourselves and create healthy boundaries.

We are not talking about a narcissistic kind of love, when we think we are better than everyone else and look down on others. We are talking about generating love from the source of the Feminine Divine, where we are accepting of ourselves and of who we are as human beings.

There is a big difference between faking self love and really transcending feminine energy.

We can tell ourselves that we are beautiful in front of the mirror, but if we don't feel it deep inside and take appropriate action, it will be of no use.

My story: When I started to date in college, my first experiences were pretty awful. I attracted young men who were not nice to me. I knew that it was not the way to be treated, but I couldn't break up with them. I had no idea how to deal with someone who was not nice, it scared me.

I didn't understand what self love and self care really meant. I had no idea about healthy boundaries. I grew up in a family where those things were natural, I didn't have to stand up for myself. I was safe and protected.

However, as I quickly learned, the world was different from my little family cocoon. Through being disrespected, I had to learn self respect.

I had a lot of work to do. I realized that the only way I could create the life that I wanted was by working on myself. Growing my self-worth and self-love had to be the priority if I was to have any meaningful relationships.

We must do the deep work of learning how to love, nurture and connect to ourselves on an emotional level from a place of love, not fear. Only then, when we look in the mirror, we will see the truth of our beautiful spirit reflected back to us.

When we feel whole inside, we don't need a constant stream of outside praise and compliments to make us feel good. We know we can give that to ourselves anytime.

In order to give to others, we must love ourselves first.

We forget about this simple wisdom often, and this is what creates unhappiness in our lives.

When we begin the day with loving ourselves first by taking care of our physical, emotional, and spiritual needs, we enable immense

gratitude and value from within. We honor who we are, first and foremost.

This shift from fear-based thoughts to those of love towards ourselves changes our energetic field and changes how everyone else perceives us.

If we feel that our boss is undervaluing us, our children are taking advantage of us, or our boyfriend/husband is not paying attention, it is because we stopped loving ourselves at the core of our being.

When we cut the energy supply that feeds us, we are not the only ones that feel it. Everyone else feels it too.

When everyone stops paying attention to us, we try harder to please, get bitter, or shut down. If we shift the focus to deep within ourselves instead of appeasing everyone around us, we find our own source of power.

Once we connect to who we are as beautiful and loving beings, everyone else picks up that energy and treats us accordingly.

If your relationships constantly fall through or your kids won't listen to you, it is because you have forgotten about you. You are not appreciating and loving yourself first.

We are all energetic beings and we can sense other people's value depending on how much they value themselves.

It is very important to develop and acknowledge our own value, as the quality of our life depends on it.

Discovering who we are can be really fun and exciting. By learning the secrets to finding your own beauty using the principles laid out in this book, you will feel like you are in the driver's seat of your life.

Your self-esteem, your confidence and your allure will become the underlying forces of your being. You will express beauty beyond measure and glow in a magnificent way for everyone to notice.

In order to grow that sacred space, we must learn to fine tune our emotional wellbeing and consciously live from a place of love.

This means that fear-based emotions like anger, jealousy, and hate must be kept in check. We cannot let such emotions dictate how we treat ourselves and others.

This isn't to say that we can't feel anger ever again, we will and it's ok. We have to learn to move those emotions through our body quickly so they don't stick around and poison us from the inside.

LOVE AND FEAR

For far too long we have been confused about who we are.

Not being who we truly are means living in fear. And living in fear drains our beauty and disconnects us from the Feminine Divine Energy.

A fear-driven life is what creates a feeling of misery and depression. When we live in fear, we live in lack. We constantly try to feed our insecurities through the outside world.

We abuse our bodies and our emotional wellbeing by making decisions from a place of anxiety. We fear that we might get fat if we quit smoking, so we keep smoking incredibly toxic fumes that slowly kill our bodies.

Or we might be afraid of not being liked so we stay in a relationship that makes us unhappy or even unsafe. We don't venture out to try to find something better.

Fear has become a way of life for many of us. We don't even notice how deeply ingrained it has become in our DNA.

We love temporarily, and then go back to living in fear full time.

It's not our fault. We have been programmed by our cultural upbringing.

We learn to feel fear to protect ourselves from danger. Toddlers learn not to touch the stove because it is hot. We learn to be afraid of dogs, if we were ever bitten by one. We become fearful if we are told to be careful all the time, "Don't do this, don't do that, you might get hurt."

Getting out of a fear-based mindset requires reprogramming our basic survival skills. Unless we consciously work on it, we have no idea how to do it.

Much more often we run to the doctor for that prescription of Zoloft or Adderall instead. We want to feel fully engaged with life, but we don't know how else to do it.

We are living a conditioned life no different than a hamster spinning in a wheel. We don't think much about our daily actions and why things are the way they are.

We forget how powerful we really are, because fear takes hold of our minds. Fear makes us forget to live from a place of love that nurtures our beauty and bliss.

Somewhere along our path, we lose control. We cannot handle our emotional burden any longer, so we decide to find ways to numb it out either by eating, drinking, smoking, or taking prescription drugs. But that is like putting a bandaid on a bleeding wound. We are not fixing the root cause of our problems.

No wonder we are so unhappy.

We as women live much better now than in our turbulent past, yet some of us feel so utterly miserable that we need to take antidepressants just to function.

We have an overabundance of goods and services, but we still struggle to be happy. We get lost, because we are no longer in touch with ourselves and our Feminine Divine.

We are no longer comfortable sharing ourselves as beautiful, powerful beings, because we think no one cares to listen to our deep cries for help. We think that no one wants to see our vulnerabilities. We forget to ask for help.

We settle into a life that is unworthy of our divine nature.

Our inner voice is put on mute, and the stereotypes of society drive our decision-making every minute of the day.

By connecting to our Feminine Divine Energy, we are opening up a new source of comfort and an infinite amount of wisdom and inspiration.

Our emotional well-being should not depend on our boss's bad mood, or our child's temper tantrum.

The pattern of using various substances to control our emotional states has made us more addicted and less at peace. So obviously it is not working.

We need change.

The most powerful change comes from within. All the happiness you desire is already inside you.

Our ability to use emotion (aka our women's superpower) is a very efficient way to tap into the Feminine Divine Energy.

Love is the most powerful of all emotions. When we are in a state of love, we can easily tell which emotions are good for our wellbeing and which ones should be released.

By using love instead of fear as our main emotion, we transform our inner and outer beauty at the same time.

Spiritual Beauty has an incredible effect on our physical form. Everything in the Universe is composed of energy, including beauty. *Therefore, even physical beauty can be changed with the energy of love.*

So you are not only making your life a happier one, but you are also making yourself much more attractive in the process. Living from a place of love takes practice and patience, but it is the only way to live a happy and fulfilling life.

Nurturing the emotions of love will lead the way to infinite beauty and an overabundance of joy.

BREAKING THE OVER-ATTACHMENT

We have a tendency to over-attach to others in unhealthy ways to justify our need for control, but we shouldn't be controlling of others.

We over-attach and don't even realize that it makes us unhappy.

When we are attached to others, we take on their emotional states, whether good or bad. This means that we are not only processing our own feelings, we are also adding someone else's on top. This makes us very confused and unbalanced.

Of course, there is a difference between a healthy attachment that is intimate and bonding, and an attachment gone awry where one person is trying to control the other, or both.

When we over-attach, a connection between two people starts to become negative.

When we over-attach by trying to hold on to someone, we give our power away and become the ones being controlled.

We all have experienced a situation when we really like someone and they don't have the same feelings towards us, yet what do we do? We keep liking them and suffering at the same time because of our attachment to this person.

So instead of focusing on ourselves and what we can control, we give our power away and hope for the best.

My story: As a continuation of my earlier story in this chapter, I often found myself having patterns of over-attachment to other people. Whether it was my best friend or a boyfriend, I would commit so much to a relationship that I would easily lose my own sense of self. This led me into toxic situations, and made me feel depleted and used.

These patterns repeated enough for me to realize that I had to stop running away from myself. I had to accept myself and really love who I am, without relying on some external source to complete me.

As I began to discover myself, and work on things that made me happy, I became comfortable in my own skin. I felt I was enough to be loved as me. I am continuously working on creating healthy boundaries that people respect while also attracting people who are right for me.

A few attachments that are unhealthy can seriously affect the way we perceive ourselves, to the point that we forget we even exist as an individual.

When we over-attach, we take ourselves out of the equation. We stop being who we truly are, we forget about our own beauty, our own identity.

We stop the flow of our own energy, because we think that the other person is more important, so we focus on them.

However, if the other person does not respond in the same way, we lose energy and as a result become very unhappy.

It is not the other person's responsibility to make us happy. It was our decision to give our power away and forget about our own happiness in the first place.

Breaking unhealthy attachments and learning how to create meaningful relationships without sacrificing our own being is possible, and it is necessary if we want to be truly fulfilled.

We have been taught that someone is supposed to make us happy. Someone is supposed to come and solve all our problems aka "The Prince."

We watch Pretty Woman and other romantic chick flicks that sell the illusion that we are only valuable if we are liked by someone. That we need someone else to see our true potential.

Don't get me wrong, I love those movies, but only for their entertainment value.

This illusion makes us feel like we are not whole as we are. So we spend our lives looking for someone to make us feel whole, because we have been taught that we are not enough.

We should look within, instead of constantly trying to find external recognition. We already have all the ingredients inside of us to make us happy and successful. These are infinite amounts of confidence, security, love, and beauty. And we need to learn how to find and nurture these amazing qualities within ourselves.

So how do we do that?

We must learn how to give to ourselves before we give to others.

We must learn what is good for us instead of draining or depleting us. The secret word here is "happiness."

Following your bliss is the priority, as our emotional well-being is at the core of who we are as women. And if that emotional center is forgotten, we wither and become invisible to everyone else.

The Aura

Being happy means being energetically attuned to your own frequency, to your own uniqueness.

When this energy flows from within, it creates a magnetic attraction to all that you desire.

This energy creates a field around your body called the aura. Your auric field can be large or small and run in different colors. It all depends on your inner state of being and how well you are tapping into your true source of Feminine Divine Energy.

Your aura is what makes you magnetic to others. Very few people can see the aura, but most will feel it. We are energetic beings and we pick up on other people's energy without even knowing.

If we know how to create a healthy aura, we can feel good about how people will respond to us.

A healthy aura means that we are aware of our emotional states and are connected to our true selves, our Feminine Divine Energy.

When our aura is not healthy, we feel emotionally and physically drained, stressed, sad, depressed, or angry. We are not aware of who we are and this leads to further weakening of our aura.

When our aura is weak, it shrinks in size and becomes thinner. With a weak aura, we are more likely to absorb the negativity of others and feel invisible to others.

When our aura is big and healthy, it radiates a glowing energy that makes us very charismatic and attractive to others.

By working on our energy field we can create instant beauty and radiance. All we have to do is go within.

Going within means tapping into your Feminine Divine Energy, finding out what makes you come alive, what makes you glow.

Within our unique soul is a treasure chest of talents, abilities, and desires, that we often overlook.

What makes you smile? What makes you feel alive? What makes you feel joy? Do you know?

If we don't know, we are not living a life full of love, joy, and abundance.

To not know what truly inspires you, is to not know the beauty you possess.

It can be a walk along the ocean shore that warms your soul and brings a soft smile of contentment. It can be having dinner with people that you treasure. It can be painting in your lush garden.

The beauty of your soul comes out from inspiration and fulfilment of your deep desires.

LEVEL 4 ACTIVATION PRACTICE:

- LIVE FROM A PLACE OF POSITIVE ("THE 33 LOVE LIST")

  - ❏ Write 33 things that you are good at and love about yourself aka "The 33 Love List." It can be something as minute as doodling on a piece of paper while you talk on the phone.

1_____	12_____	23_____
2_____	13_____	24_____
3_____	14_____	25_____
4_____	15_____	26_____
5_____	16_____	27_____
6_____	17_____	28_____
7_____	18_____	29_____
8_____	19_____	30_____
9_____	20_____	31_____
10_____	21_____	32_____
11_____	22_____	33_____

- PRACTICE ACCEPTANCE

  - ❏ Write five things about yourself that you find irritate you the most and compare them to the "The 33 Love List." Then you will realize how many more things there are that you actually love about yourself. So change your focus to what you love every time you think bad things about yourself.

    1_____

    2_____

    3_____

4_____

5_____

- ANCHOR THE EMOTION OF LOVE

  ❏ Remember an activity or a place that created positive feelings in you. Write down the activity/place and the feeling. While you are in that state of bliss, hold your wrist or do some kind of movement that you remember to "anchor" this feeling. Every time you want to feel that state of bliss, do that motion with your hand, for example, hold your right wrist and it will activate those feelings.

Activity/Place	Feeling	Anchoring movement
Ex: Laying on a white beach in Maldives	Happy & peaceful	Holding index finger and thumb together
_____	_____	_____
_____	_____	_____
_____	_____	_____
_____	_____	_____
_____	_____	_____

• FIND YOURSELF AGAIN

☐ Make a list of 10 things that are important to you and only you. It could be what you always wanted to do, wear, eat, or travel to. Do these things by yourself without asking for permission or needing to do them with anyone else. Do it for yourself only. This will bring you back to knowing what it's like to be in your own energies.

1 _____

2 _____

3 _____

4 _____

5 _____

6 _____

7 _____

8 _____

9 _____

10 _____

Level 5

SPEAKING YOUR TRUTH

Chakra: 5th, Throat
Color: Light Blue

5ᵀᴴ CHAKRA AFFIRMATIONS

"I speak highly of myself and others."

"I communicate honestly with others from a place of love."

How we communicate with ourselves and others comes from the fifth level. Our intentions with every word we think or speak manifests in our lives through our fifth, or throat chakra.

If we talk negatively, we create a fear-based reality. If we hold the words of love, we create a life of harmony and the freedom to express our authentic selves.

SILENCING THE CRITIC WITHIN

There are stressors that come from the outside, but often we create them ourselves.

We can have negative thoughts that we are used to playing over and over in our heads, such as, 'I'm not good enough,' 'I'm ugly,' 'I'm miserable.' The list goes on.

Negative thoughts congest our mind and keep us stuck in a negative cycle, which prevents the flow of Feminine Divine Energy.

We are often unaware of what we say to ourselves, because we forget to listen. Our mind can become so repetitive that we wonder why we can't feel happy or beautiful. Well it's because we keep putting ourselves down every chance we get with our own thoughts.

We blame everyone for our shortcomings, but sometimes we are our worst enemy. Our mind that is.

How often do we give ourselves compliments, as opposed to finding things that are wrong with us? What we say to ourselves matters.

Western beauty culture revolves around hiding flaws, but in Ukraine, the main concept is to show your best self. At first it might seem like the same thing, however, it requires a totally different mindset.

Western beauty teaches us that we are made of flaws, which creates unhealthy patterns and insecurities. We constantly think there is something wrong with us and we need to hide it.

On the contrary, in Ukrainian culture, women think about how to enhance their best features. They are not obsessed with their flaws. This kind of thinking creates a confident woman.

My story: My first business venture in my early twenties happened to be a clothing boutique in Ukraine. Little did I realize (before the concept of this book was born) that this was the perfect case study of Ukrainian women.

I got to know their tastes and desires; how they viewed their bodies; their self-esteem. Dressing them was a totally different experience than what I had imagined.

The women that came to my store were only buying clothes that looked amazing. It had to be exclusive, looking and fitting perfectly. They would not settle for less. The level of expectation was that of a couture house, yet my prices were far far less.

What Ukrainian women were shopping for was for something to elevate their beauty, not just a thing to wear.

I was comparing their shopping habits to mine. I digested my closet and realized I had a lot of clothes, but nothing to wear. I would buy a shirt in five different colors..etc. Meanwhile, Ukrainian women spent a lot less on their clothes and bought only a few good pieces, but those few made them look incredible.

Ukrainian women wear clothes that accentuate their figure in the most flattering way. They will ONLY buy clothes that look amazing. They will not invest in clothes that hide their body, no matter what their shape or size.

They use makeup to enhance their natural beauty, not to cover it up with layers of foundation. They believe that you must give room for your true self to shine, playing up your uniqueness and not focusing on flaws.

When we focus on our best features, our flaws seem to get smaller and disappear. They lose importance in our thoughts.

Another important truth is to understand that when we criticize others, we are also criticizing ourselves.

We have a tendency as women to gossip. It is a universal phenomena, but one that is centered in negativity.

Imagine if gossip was replaced with positive and supportive comments about one another. How would that reflect on our life?

We would, in a short time, be able to connect to our Feminine Divine. Because instead of negativity, we would flow from a place of love.

SPEAKING YOUR TRUTH

Which brings me to another important principle - speaking your truth. It is so hard to know what we should say and what we should not say. Sometimes we don't say things for fear of hurting someone, but in reality we are hurting ourselves. We keep things inside, let them fester into anger, depression and resentment. And then we blow up on the people that mean so much to us.

Alternatively, sometimes we say too much of what we should not say. The important concept to understand is that we must gauge our ways of expression, so that it comes from love, not fear.

This goes back to an understanding of our emotional wellness. We should say things that heal us and heal others. Sometimes it's not what other people want to hear and might be very hard to say. However, we understand that we have to speak our truth so that we don't keep it bottled up inside. The key is to find balance.

Oftentimes, we hide our true feelings from others for fear of being rejected. We don't say "I love you" or "I miss you" often enough. But if we do feel this love inside, then we must share it. This is vulnerability.

Vulnerability

Vulnerability does not mean disempowerment. Vulnerability is strength, because it is speaking what's coming from your heart.

If we are vulnerable, we are genuine and honest with ourselves, and that is something we want to aspire to. It is scary to be vulnerable when you have been hurt and taken for granted, but what is the alternative?

The Feminine Divine flows from love and, if we want to be feminine, we have to let vulnerability be a strength in our lives.

The more we practice this concept of vulnerability, the more we become confident and present with who we are as soul beings.

We open ourselves up to allow love from the outside to fill us, because we are not afraid and are not hiding who we are. Often we diminish ourselves because we feel that who we are is not acceptable. We hide our true power, our potential, in order to fit in, but we are all unique beings and our strength is in our uniqueness.

As I have learned from Ukrainian culture, being feminine is expressing your uniqueness. To be truly beautiful and vulnerable is also letting your unique self shine brightly.

When we come from our vulnerability and uniqueness, we are joyous and fulfilled. Joy comes from living in your truth and not being afraid of what others think of you or say about you. Your femininity comes alive when you live your purpose, because it is your divine birthright.

LEVEL 5 ACTIVATION PRACTICE

- SILENCE THE CRITIC WITHIN

  ❐ Choose one full day out of the week where you only use compliments towards yourself and others. No criticism of any kind.

  List compliments that you will say:

  _____

  _____

  _____

  _____

  _____

  _____

- SPEAK YOUR TRUTH

  ❐ Find someone you have been hiding your true feelings from and practice actually saying them to them.

  Write down what you will say and to whom:

  Person   **What You Will Say**

  _____   _____

  _____   _____

  _____   _____

Level 6

MASTER YOUR MIND FOR FEMININE POWER

Chakra: 6th, Third Eye
Color: Indigo

6ᵀᴴ CHAKRA AFFIRMATIONS

"I monitor my thoughts closely. I am in control of my mind."

"I change my habits by trying new things."

From the place of the third eye, or the sixth chakra, comes our connection to our psyche. From this place, which is the sixth level, we learn that we are not our mind, we have a mind.

We learn to either control our thoughts, or let our thoughts control us. We form habits and learn how to break them. We embrace the new and release the old that no longer serves our higher purpose.

Think of your whole life and how it has made you who you are today. Your mind has been wired a certain way, it took many years. This programming is strong, but it can be changed.

BREAKING THE AUTOPILOT

Scientific literature suggests that it takes at least 21 days to change a habit.

Our habits define how we live our lives. They rule how we interact with the world and its stressors. When we look at our reaction to stress as a set of habits, we can find ways to solve it by taking little steps everyday, for at least 21 days. For example, if we continuously keep reacting to a certain person in a negative way, we should pause and think about WHY we react this way.

When we look deeper into the reasons why that person is bothering us, we might realize that there is something within us that is actually bothering us, and that person is only a trigger for it.

Everyday for 21 days you can take a moment to be aware of how you react to something stressful and change that one little reaction. Little by little, you start to realize that your life is becoming less stressful and more peaceful.

Journaling

One way you can learn about your thinking patterns is by journaling. I have found journaling to be an amazing tool to organize my mind and I highly recommend it.

Find some daily alone time, even if it is only for 15 minutes, to write everything that is in your head, your thoughts, your worries, your to do lists. Write them all down.

Try to keep your journal for at least 21 days.

You will be amazed how much this little exercise will help you get connected to your mind. The purpose of this is to become aware of our mind chatter, so that we can recognize when we are becoming reactive or negative.

We have spent years and years creating these negative systems that run our mind, so do not expect that all of your problems will magically disappear overnight.

Pave a New Road

It takes time to rewire our brains. Imagine you walked the same road for years, and it formed an embedded pattern from your footprints.

You can clearly see this road now, because you have travelled the same road day after day.

One day you decide to take another way. There is no road yet, it is a field, but the more you walk this new way, the more it starts to become a road, much like the old one.

As you keep walking on the new road, the old one gets overgrown with weeds and eventually disappears into a field again.

Our brains work in a similar way. The roads are our habits, and the thoughts are the footsteps that make the road.

When we step on the road, we reinforce a certain habit with our thoughts.

In order to weaken and erase our old habits, the "old road," we must begin thinking new thoughts and taking new action to pave the "new road."

Expanding Your Horizons

If we want to change our minds, we must think differently.

Thinking differently means not passively following and reacting to everything around us. It is about being aware of our thoughts and then choosing the best ones to reach our goals.

Try a new experience that is out of your comfort zone. For example, if you have never tried belly dancing, take a class even if you have no idea what you are doing. Laugh and enjoy the process. You are not only learning how to move your hips to the music, you are also connecting more deeply to yourself.

Challenge yourself to see how far you can stretch your mind. It might be reading a book that is outside your usual genre. If you've always preferred novels, read a self-help book, or vice versa. This seems so basic, but it really works for retraining your mind.

My story: "When I was studying a lot of science in high school and in college, I wondered why I needed to remember so much. Would I ever use this later in my life? What was the point?

It was only years after finishing my studies that I realized that studying in itself was making me expand my mind. It made me think about the world in a much more open way. I began to see unlimited possibilities and also understand people in a new way."

This is the way we have to look at beauty and femininity. ***Beauty does not just happen. It is something we learn. And by learning it, we expand our beauty consciousness and take it to another level.***

When we are trying to learn a new skill in any subject, we are changing and evolving. This gives us a new level of understanding about the world. By studying anything, we are creating a mind that is open to other possibilities.

We must be open-minded to grasp the concept of inner beauty, which is Feminine Divine Energy.

We have been so used to seeing beauty just on a physical level, that seeing it differently can be quite a stretch. Therefore, it is important to keep our minds flexible by taking on new skills and challenges.

We may not be comfortable with new information at first, so we dismiss it. However, if it does not work the first time, the second or third time might be the charm.

My story: "There was a time after I finished college, when I wasn't sure who I wanted to be or what I wanted to do. I wrote out a list of careers that sounded interesting and went about trying them. One career was to be a lawyer, so I went ahead and started studying for the LSATs.

The first time I ever opened the LSAT practice book, I could not even understand a sentence, let alone solve a logical problem. Logic, as I realized, was really not "my thing." My educational background was much stronger in science, but I persisted.

I kept reading the same problems over and over, until something surprising happened. All of a sudden, I began to understand the language of law!

I ended up crossing law school off my list, but the process to get into law school in itself was so interesting and expansive. My confidence went up and I felt like I could do anything. I also realized that I didn't want to be a lawyer, which meant I was one step closer to finding out who I wanted to be."

How often do we tell ourselves "Oh, that was such a waste of time!" However, in reality, everything is an invaluable life experience, if we have the right attitude.

We can focus on why something didn't work out, or we can focus on what we learned from that situation and how it changed us.

My story: "For me, going from not understanding a word of LSATs to really getting it was an accomplishment of its own. It made me realize that I can learn anything I set my mind to, that there was nothing I could not grasp.

It was quite liberating and empowering, and I used that uplifting energy to propel me to my next career on the list.

So I kept crossing things off my list. For some people it might have seemed that I was just failing at everything I did, but to me it was quite the opposite. By trying to discover which career was true to my heart, I was also discovering who I was in the process.

It opened up a new dimension within me, a pathway to dig deeper within. I was learning what my true hopes and desires were. It was all because I was trying things that did not make me comfortable at first, but later I understood their purpose."

Our fears stall our development and keep us from finding out who we truly are. We are afraid that if we do 'dig deeper,' we will find something ugly and unpleasant.

So, at a certain point we stop developing. We stop trying things that make us uncomfortable. We become creatures of habit.

We think that we already know what we are capable of, but is it ever possible to reach our limit in potential? We think not.

If we have infinite potential in our lives, we also have that same infinite potential in our beauty.

Beauty is who we are, truly. By discovering who we are, we discover our beauty and what makes us unique.

Fear is what stops us from truly knowing ourselves. It paralyzes our talents and our dreams.

We must practice opening a new dimension by learning what we do not yet know. It is by making unfamiliar, familiar, and by making uncomfortable, comfortable. It can be challenging and scary at times, because we are opening more of our heart and our vulnerabilities.

Emotions that have been neglected and repressed can come out and it can be overwhelming.

However, this is a natural process of getting to know oneself. It is very important to be present and pay attention to what our mind will say. For example, "What will others think of me?" or "If I fail, I will look silly."

By not learning and expanding in order to "avoid failure," we are denying ourselves the truth of knowing our full potential.

When we are not fully present and aware of who we are, we become victims of other people's opinions/manipulations and run the risk of losing autonomy over our lives.

LEVEL 6 ACTIVATION PRACTICE:

- BREAK THE AUTOPILOT

  ☐ JOURNALING

  Go out and get yourself a beautiful journal to write in. Something that really catches your eye. Start writing whatever comes to your mind, even if it is just for one minute. Repeat this every day for at least 21 days. The action of writing down your mind chatter helps you think clearly. It also helps you to realize what feelings you have been holding back and why, as they will pour out naturally. Write from a place of non-judgement, where you allow yourself to just be.

  ☐ PAVE A NEW ROAD

  Whenever you want to change a habit and feel stuck, write down what you want to replace it with. By focusing on developing the new habit, the old one will fade with time. List the negative associations of the old habit. In the next column list the positive associations of the new habit.

	Bad Habit – negative associations	Replacement Habit – positive associations
Ex:	Late night snacking - weight gain - heartburn - sleeplessness - being tired in the morning - feeling out of control	No snacking after dinner - better weight management - better sleep - more energy in the morning - feeling good about yourself
	_____	_____
	_____	_____

_____   _____

_____   _____

❑ EXPAND YOUR HORIZONS

Find a class/activity that will challenge you in a physical or mental way and engage in it for at least 3 weeks. You will be able to shift your thinking, pave a new road and expand your mind.

Write down five things you want to do to expand your horizons:

1_____

2_____

3_____

4_____

5_____

Level 7

YOU ARE A GODDESS

Chakra: 7th, Crown
Color: Purple

7TH CHAKRA AFFIRMATIONS

"I am a Goddess. It is my birthright."

Your connection to the Divine, the crown or seventh chakra, is where heaven meets earth. It is where we can connect to the invisible force that is within us all. We can channel beauty, art, ideas through this energetic center.

It is a place of opening up to higher consciousness and working through our illusions of thought. It is where we learn to understand that there is more to life than meets the eye. From this place we see magic and miracles happen.

Once you work through the previous six levels up to the seventh level of the crown chakra, you reach the height of your Feminine Divine. You now understand what it truly means to be feminine.

HONOR YOUR DIVINITY

To strengthen your connection to Feminine Divine Energy, read the rest of this chapter to remind yourself of who you are. Take great pride in being a woman and honor yourself with love and divinity at all times.

You are now in the flow.

You are aware of your greatest power and greatest potential.

You do your daily tasks with ease. Femininity is a part of your life. Your energy is completely transformed, and you have the tools to keep yourself on track.

A woman is naturally connected to God and to everything in this world. A feminine woman is a goddess, whose purpose in this world is to live from the spirit of the Feminine Divine Energy.

When you become a goddess, you live and breathe femininity. Everyday, as the sun rises, you give love to this world and, as the sun sets, you fill yourself back up with that love.

No matter how much you give, a goddess is always full of love.

No matter how much you have seen of the things that have hurt you, a goddess is always full of compassion.

No matter how far you have been away from your true self, you know your goddess ways. It's only a matter of a thought that brings you back home.

Your home lies in your Feminine Divine. From here you grow, from here you flourish.

When obstacles come your way, you remember that you are a Goddess made of love, that you have the power to heal yourself and others.

You have the power to change your world. By changing your world, you are changing the entire world.

When you look deep within and see your beautiful soul, your true strength is to show everyone who you are.

It is not for you to see like everyone else. It is to inspire everyone else to see you.

You were born a Goddess. There is nothing you have to do to earn this.

You are a woman, a friend, a sister, a mother, but don't forget that first and foremost you are a Goddess.

You are the Feminine Divine, and the whole world belongs to you.

The world which you created and have the power to create.

You hold the magic of the Universe under your fingertips.

With a snap of a finger you bless the world with love and peace.

"Be in your true power, Feminine Divine
Be who you were born to be - a shining star,
a drop of rain, a wind of change, an earthquake to awake

This is your time, you are awakened now

You are so free and so alive
Step into your power, step into your strength,
Feminine Divine, release your heavy pain"

By nurturing peace and harmony from within in the way of the Feminine Divine, it spills out onto the world coloring all in its path with love and light.

"A woman that is lost, in need of inspiration
To light the way to find herself again
She is so strong but thinks she's weak
Her tears aren't wasted

She is as bright as sun
And all bask in her rays

A woman of great intellect
and feminine compassion
She gathers smiles
All across the scattered sea

She is a voice of beauty
Love grows through her kindness
She finds herself
So she can give the world
That only she can see"

\- Tetyana

LEVEL 7 ACTIVATION PRACTICE

- HONOR YOUR DIVINITY

  ☐ Somewhere in your home, build an altar consisting of your most precious things. It can be flower petals, crystals or whatever is the most dear to you. Start your day with honoring yourself and your connection to the Feminine Divine. This will remind you to live your higher purpose every day.

FEMININE ENERGY ACTIVATION CHART

Level 1 The Gateway To The Feminine Divine	
Connect To Other Women	"I am surrounded by women who love me and whom I honor."
Be In Nature	"I am part of the natural world. It inspires and invigorates me."
Nourish The Body	"I connect to the Feminine Divine Energy by nurturing my body through food."
Level 2 **Our True Source Of Beauty**	
Cultivate Feminine Energies	"I honor the masculine and feminine energies within me." "I love and respect men."
Focus On Uniqueness Spiritual Beauty (The "Inside-Out Effect")	"I am a source of infinite beauty. It flows easily from me." "I embrace my uniqueness, as it makes me beautiful." "All I need is already within me."

Level 3 Building Beauty That Lasts	
Create Beauty By Feeling It	"I feel good therefore I am beautiful."
Build Confidence Through Kindness	"I empower myself by living from a place of kindness and treating others the same."
Catch Your Stress Patterns	"I find better ways to deal with life upsets."
Level 4 The Beauty Mindset - Loving Yourself First	
Live From A Place Of Positive ("The 33 Love List")	"I go through life from a place of love."
Practice Acceptance	"I love and accept myself exactly as I am."
Anchor The Emotion Of Love	"When I do ____ (fill in the blank), I feel happy and I also choose to feel it now."
Find Yourself Again (break the over-attachment)	"My own needs matter. I choose to do what makes me feel good."
Level 5 Speaking Your Truth	
Silence The Critic Within ("Positivity Gossip")	"I speak highly of myself and others."
Speak Your Truth	"I communicate honestly with others from a place of love."

Level 6 Mind Habits And Beauty	
Break The Autopilot	"I monitor my thoughts closely. I am in control of my mind." "I change my habits by trying new things."
Level 7 You Are A Goddess / Evolving Your Intuition	
Honor Your Divinity	"I am a Goddess. It is my birthright."

ACKNOWLEDGEMENTS

I would like to thank my main editor and writing coach Gay Walley for her guidance. Her belief, encouragement, and inspiration kept me going through many of life's ups and downs. It was essential in writing this book.

Also many thanks to my dear friends and family who encouraged me to keep going. You have supported me tremendously and I am very honored and thankful for everything you have done. I could not have done it without you.